FOX RIVER VALLEY PLD
3 1783 00478 0551
P9-BZD-061

Carly Rae Jepsen

By Kelly McNiven

Crabtree Publishing Company
www.crabtreebooks.com

Crabtree Publishing Company

www.crabtreebooks.com

Author: Kelly McNiven
Publishing plan research and development: Reagan Miller
Photo research: Crystal Sikkens
Editor: Kathy Middleton
Proofreader and Indexer: Wendy Scavuzzo
Designer: Ken Wright
Production coordinator and prepress technician: Ken Wright
Print coordinator: Margaret Amy Salter

Every effort has been made to trace copyright holders and to obtain their permission for use of copyright material. The authors and publishers would be pleased to rectify any error or omission in future editions. All the Internet addresses given in this book were correct at the time of going to press. The author and publishers regret any inconvenience caused if addresses have changed or sites have ceased to exist, but can accept no responsibility for any such changes.

Photographs:
Associated Press: cover, pages 19, 23
Getty Images: Rich Lam: page 7; Jim Ross/Stringer: page 9; George Dimentel/WireImage: page 10; Jeff Kravitz: page 13; WireImage: page 20; Fox Image Collection: page 24
Keystone Press: zumapress.com: pages 4, 15, 16, 17, 18, 25, 26, 28; Entertainment Pictures: page 8; Tonya Wise/AdMedia: page 14; Mavrixphoto.com: page 21; Carv/AKM-GSI: page 22; wenn.com: page 27
Shutterstock: Paul Smith/Featureflash: page 1; Featureflash: page 12; Joe Seer: page 5; Route66: page 6
Wikimedia Commons: Brendan: page 11

Library and Archives Canada Cataloguing in Publication

McNiven, Kelly, author
Carly Rae Jepsen / Kelly McNiven.

(Superstars!)
Includes index.
Issued in print and electronic formats.
ISBN 978-0-7787-0021-0 (bound).--ISBN 978-0-7787-0042-5 (pbk.).-- ISBN 978-1-4271-9383-4 (pdf).--ISBN 978-1-4271-9377-3 (html)

1. Jepsen, Carly Rae, 1985- --Juvenile literature.
2. Singers--Canada--Biography--Juvenile literature.
I. Title. II. Series: Superstars! (St. Catharines, Ont.)

ML3930.J545M16 2013 j782.42164092 C2013-905229-1
C2013-905230-5

Library of Congress Cataloging-in-Publication Data

McNiven, Kelly.
Carly Rae Jepsen / Kelly McNiven.
pages cm. -- (Superstars!)
Includes index.
ISBN 978-0-7787-0021-0 (reinforced library binding : alk. paper) -- ISBN 978-0-7787-0042-5 (pbk. : alk. paper) -- ISBN 978-1-4271-9383-4 (electronic pdf) -- ISBN 978-1-4271-9377-3 (electronic html)
1. Jepsen, Carly Rae, 1985---Juvenile literature. 2. Singers--Canada--Biography--Juvenile literature. I. Title.

ML3930.J47M36 2014
782.42164092--dc23
[B]

2013036160

Crabtree Publishing Company

www.crabtreebooks.com 1-800-387-7650

Printed in Canada/102013/BF20130920

Published in Canada
Crabtree Publishing
616 Welland Ave.
St. Catharines, ON
L2M 5V6

Published in the United States
Crabtree Publishing
PMB 59051
350 Fifth Avenue, 59th Floor
New York, New York 10118

Published in the United Kingdom
Crabtree Publishing
Maritime House
Basin Road North, Hove
BN41 1WR

Published in Australia
Crabtree Publishing
3 Charles Street
Coburg North
VIC 3058

CONTENTS

Words that are defined in the glossary are in bold type the first time they appear in the text.

Meet Carly!

Canadian singer-songwriter Carly Rae Jepsen rocketed to international fame during the summer of 2012 with the release of her catchy song "Call Me Maybe." With a number-one single in over 37 countries and a helping hand from pop superstar Justin Bieber, Carly has captured the attention of music fans around the world.

FAN FEVER

While Carly entertains music lovers of all ages, many of her fans are **tweens**. Carly often tweets to her fans on Twitter, calling them "Jepsies."

Carly poses with some "Jepsies" at the Q102 Springle Ball in Philadelphia, Pennsylvania.

Eyes on the Prize

Carly has won awards in countries around the world, many for her record-breaking single "Call Me Maybe." With two full-length albums under her belt, she has performed with Justin Bieber across Europe and North America and is currently **headlining** her own tour. Fans have fallen in love with Carly's girl-next-door charm and amazing voice.

Carly was named the Rising Star of 2012 at the Billboard Music Awards.

Growing Up

Carly was born on November 21, 1985, in Mission, British Columbia, Canada. She has an older brother Colin, and a younger sister named Katie. When the three siblings were young, their parents Larry and Alexandra divorced and both eventually remarried. All of Carly's parents and stepparents are teachers or principals. Encouragement from her family has helped Carly become a runaway global success today!

Inspiring Artists

From a young age, Carly loved music. She began to write and perform her own music when she was only seven years old. At age 17, Carly received her first acoustic guitar. She often performed in local cafes and pubs. As Carly grew up, her musical taste has been influenced by such superstars as Robyn and Dragonette. She also likes to listen to jazz music.

Carly grew up listening to legendary musicians such as James Taylor and Leonard Cohen (right).

Drama Queen

In high school, Carly's love of performing continued to grow. She took to the stage as the lead in several musical theater productions. She had starring roles in *Annie*, *Grease*, and *The Wiz*. After graduation, Carly moved to Victoria to attend the Canadian College of Performing Arts. While in school, Carly briefly considered following in her parents' footsteps and becoming a music teacher. Fortunately for her fans, her love of writing music was stronger and she decided to follow her dream of becoming a professional singer-songwriter.

During a hometown concert, Carly performed on the same stage where she acted in high school.

Singing the Blues

Carly was uncertain how she was going to make it as a singer. She took a series of low-paying jobs just to make ends meet. When she wasn't songwriting, she was a pastry chef's assistant, a waitress, and a nanny. She even once used her musical talents to sing her way into a bartending job. She also helped start an acoustic night at a coffee shop where she worked in Vancouver. In 2007, she was putting together a swing band when a new opportunity came knocking.

A Push Forward

Carly was ready to break into the Canadian music scene. Her former high school drama teacher encouraged her to try out for *Canadian Idol*, a reality show singing competition that featured singers from across Canada. At first, Carly was **skeptical** that reality television would be her foot in the door to a professional singing career. But after receiving a lot of encouragement, she decided to try out at the Vancouver auditions.

Ben Mulroney was the host of *Canadian Idol* for six seasons until the show ended in 2008.

She Said It

"I wasn't convinced, but my teacher said, 'The only way that any of these doors are going to open is if you knock on every single one of them. Don't decide your path. Let it decide you.'"
—On her audition for *Canadian Idol*, *carlyraemusic.com*

Making the Cut

At her audition, Carly played acoustic guitar and performed one of her original songs, "Sweet Talker." She floored the judges with her strong voice. In a **unanimous** decision, the four judges presented Carly with a golden ticket that sent her to the next round of competition in Toronto, Ontario. Still not convinced that the show would bring her fame, Carly decided that even if she lost, at least she could try to launch her career while she was in Toronto.

Canadian Idol judges (from left) promoter Jake Gold, singer Sass Jordan, manager Farley Flex, and musician Zack Werner, all helped Carly on her rise to stardom.

Coast to Coast

As the show began, Canadians quickly fell in love with Carly's folk-style singing and bubbly personality. At the end of each show, viewers would call in from coast to coast to vote on their favorite contestants. Carly covered a wide range of songs, performing everything from **reggae** to **soul** music. Carly has admitted she was a "nightmare" on the show, choosing songs which were not always easy for the show's producers to get permission for the contestants to cover. However, her choices proved successful and, although she didn't win, she finished the show in third place.

Tug of War

Shortly after *Canadian Idol* ended, Carly released her first single. She covered a classic John Denver song called "Sunshine On My Shoulders." She then signed with the music **label** Fontana/MapleMusic to record her first album *Tug of War*. Carly was proud to have written nine songs on the album, which earned her nominations for two Juno Awards and a MuchMusic Video Award. While the album was received well in Canada, Carly was still not well known in the United States or internationally.

Carly strikes a pose on the red carpet at the 2010 Juno Awards where she was nominated for New Artist of the Year and Songwriter of the Year.

The Long Way Up

In January 2009, a music video was made for the song "Tug of War" off the album with the same name. Carly also recorded her first **duet** "Sour Candy" with Josh Ramsay, the lead singer of pop band Marianas Trench. Carly struck up a friendship with the band and set out on a tour of western Canada opening for Marianas Trench, and Shiloh—another Canadian artist. She then joined Marianas Trench on the road again on their cross-country Masterpiece Theatre Tour. In 2011, Carly was signed to a new record label 604 Records, co-owned by her manager Jonathan Simkin.

Dressed in red, her favorite color, Carly performs "Tug of War" in Vancouver on Canada Day in 2010.

Growing Pains

While on tour, Carly began to feel herself being pulled in a new direction as an artist. She watched fans react to the upbeat sound of the headlining band Marianas Trench. She wanted to have the same effect on the crowd with her own songs. Carly decided it was time to take a fresh approach to her music.

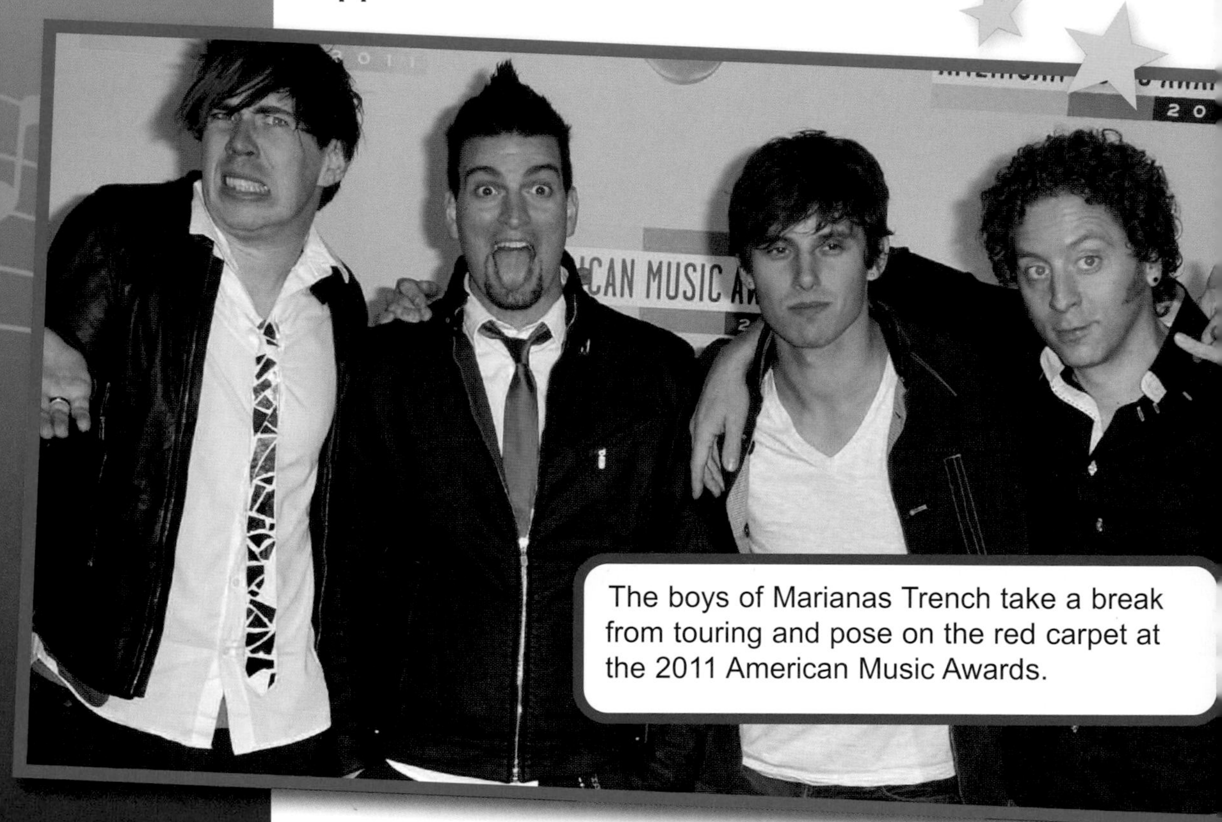

The boys of Marianas Trench take a break from touring and pose on the red carpet at the 2011 American Music Awards.

She Said It

"I saw the effect they had on the crowd, how they inspired the audience to get up and dance and that appealed to me. I wanted to create that kind of energy with my music."

–On her inspiration from Marianas Trench to take her music in a new direction, *carlyraemusic.com*

Call Me...

During the tour, Carly and her bandmate guitar player Tavish Crowe were working together on a new folk song. With some help from Josh Ramsay, himself a successful music producer, the song was reworked with a new pop twist.

Carly and Tavish Crowe are dressed to impress at the 2012 MTV European Music Awards in Germany.

Definitely!

The first time Carly played the reworked, feel-good song for her family, her aunt—known for not being a dancer—got up and started dancing. For Carly, this was an early glimpse of the lively effect her new sound would have on fans around the world. "Call Me Maybe" was released in Canada in September of 2011. The song climbed the charts and reached number one on the Canadian Hot 100 charts on February 11, 2012.

The Tweet That Changed It All

Fellow Canadian artist Justin Bieber heard "Call Me Maybe" playing on the radio while he has home for Christmas in Ontario. Impressed by Carly's sound, the mega-popstar logged onto Twitter and tweeted to his 15 million followers about the new single he had just heard: "Call me maybe by Carly Rae Jepsen is possibly the catchiest song I've ever heard." His celebrity girlfriend at the time, American singer Selena Gomez, also shared the song with her followers.

Carly and Justin pose together at the 2012 MuchMusic Video Awards in Toronto.

Mmmm Bop!

With the momentum of "Call Me Maybe" beginning to build, Carly set out on a Canadian tour in January opening for the popular brothers in Hanson on their Shout It Out World Tour! The tour included 13 shows in several major cities, including Toronto, Montreal, and Vancouver. While on the road, a hysterical phone call from her sister Katie caught Carly off guard. Katie told her Justin Bieber had just tweeted about her song!

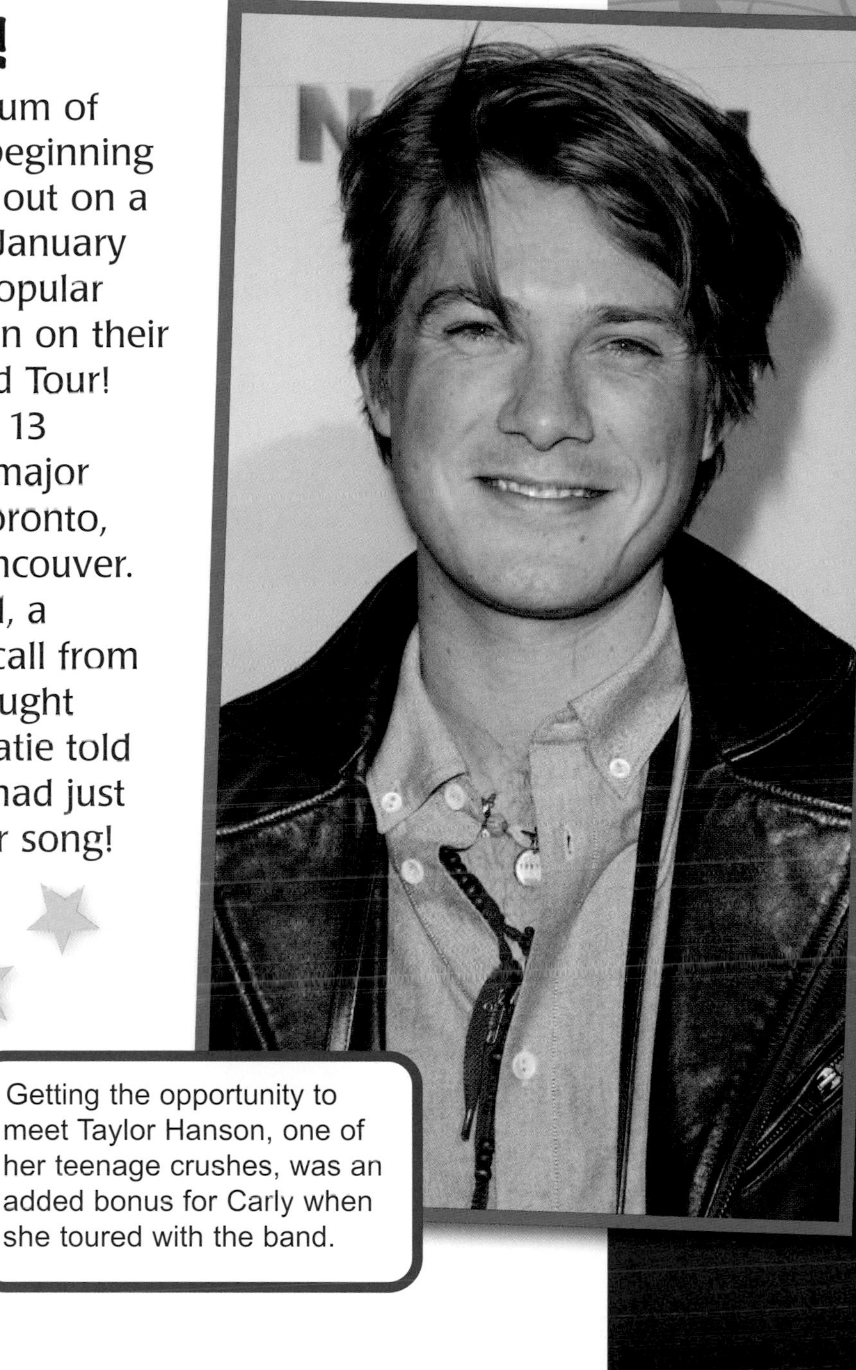

Getting the opportunity to meet Taylor Hanson, one of her teenage crushes, was an added bonus for Carly when she toured with the band.

Fame Calling

A very excited Carly was invited to Los Angeles to meet Justin, and his manager Scooter Braun. Within half an hour of meeting Justin, Carly was in the studio with him working on an acoustic duet called "Beautiful." Carly became the first official artist signed to Bieber's label School Boy Records.

Overnight Sensation

With Bieber's boost, "Call Me Maybe" went **viral**. The song became the first single by a Canadian to top U.S. charts since Justin Bieber's "Baby." The song exploded on social media with dozens of covers and **parodies** appearing on YouTube. Carly has a few personal favorites, including Justin Bieber and Selena Gomez's video lip-syncing the song with a group of friends, as well as the cookie-themed take on her catchy tune by *Sesame Street*'s Cookie Monster. Other popular covers were created by superstar Katy Perry, talk show host Jimmy Fallon, and the United States Olympic swim team. The parodies are so popular that many have received over one million views on YouTube.

Rather than "call me maybe," Cookie Monster asks viewers with a cookie to "share it maybe!"

A Sweet Treat

Valentine's Day in 2012 was a particularly sweet day for Carly. She publicly announced signing with Justin Bieber's label and also released her second album—an **EP** (extended play) album titled *Curiosity*. Carly had originally intended to release her second full-length album on that day. However, she decided a few days before the launch to only release an EP because a full-length album felt too rushed.

TOP OF THE CHARTS

"Call Me Maybe" is one of the best-selling singles of all time, with over 13 million copies sold worldwide. It was also the best-selling single of 2012 downloaded on iTunes.

While Carly toured the world with Justin, she made several media appearances to promote the *Curiosity* EP and "Call Me Maybe."

Always a Good Time!

With her whirlwind success, Carly has partnered up with many artists for duets. In 2012, she worked with Owl City to record the summer sensation "Good Time," which topped charts around the world. Rap superstar Nicki Minaj has also **remixed** Carly's song "Tonight I'm Getting Over You." Carly has said that her dream collaboration would be to work with John Mayer. She was incredibly touched when he sent her a personal note after the craze of "Call Me Maybe," saying how much he liked the song.

Carly and Owl City lead vocalist Adam Young show a New York City street packed with fans a great time during a free performance on the *Today* show in August 2012.

Believe!

Carly teamed up with Justin again as the opening act on the North American leg of his Believe world tour. She also opened for his shows in the United Kingdom and France. The tour was an incredible experience for Carly. In an interview with a British radio station, Carly described her first show opening for Bieber as a "wow, pinch me" moment and as one of her best memories of 2012. During the tour's stop in Vancouver, Carly earned extra points as a big sister when she introduced an excited Katie to Justin.

BEHIND THE MUSIC

Carly's bandmates include Tavish Crowe on guitar, Solomon Standing on bass, Nik Pesut on drums, and Jared Manierka on keyboards.

Justin joined Carly on stage in London to sing "Call Me Maybe" during radio station Capital FM's Summertime Ball.

The Future Is Bright!

In September of 2012, less than six months after "Call Me Maybe" took the world by storm, Carly's next album *Kiss* was released. Carly helped write most of the songs on the album. *Kiss* sold over 46,000 copies in its first week in stores and earned Carly multiple nominations at the Grammy and Juno Awards.

DEAR DIARY

Most of Carly's songs are on matters of the heart, and she uses inspiration from her own life and others in her **lyrics**. She keeps her ideas written down in over 60 unfinished diaries!

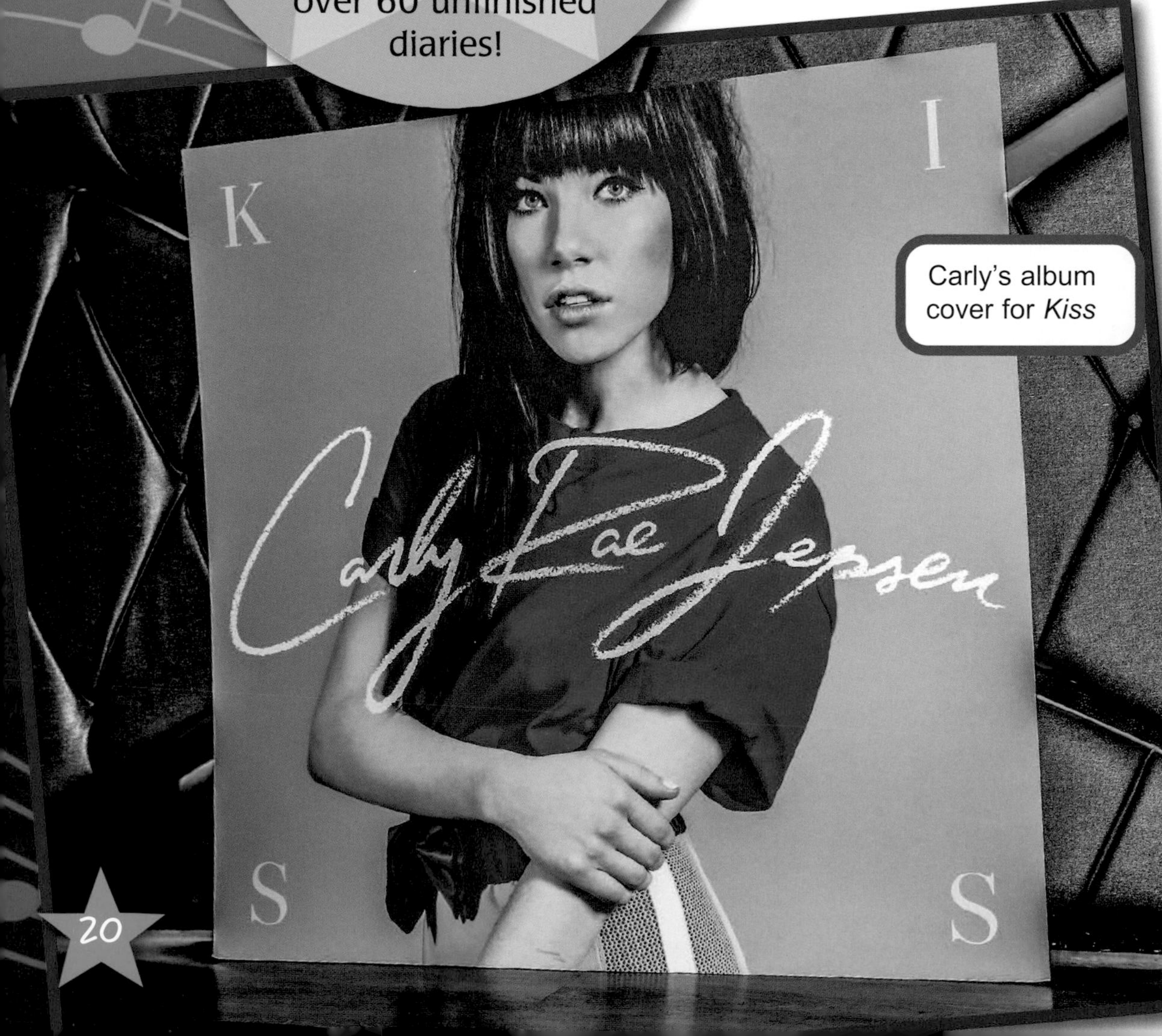

Carly's album cover for *Kiss*

Love in the Air

While working on the "This Kiss" track for her new album, sparks flew when Carly met American singer-songwriter Matthew Koma. In early 2013, the two began dating. The two performers make time in their busy schedules and world travels to spend quality time together at least once a week. Carly and Matthew have both expressed an interest in **collaborating** on their music somewhere down the road.

Carly and Matthew walk hand in hand on a romantic beach getaway in Miami, Florida.

She Said It

"I have a life-long fascination with the subject of love. When I meet people for the first time and we get past the surface-y conversations, I am always dying to know what their 'love story' is. Everyone has one. It's not always happy, but it's a story, and I like putting it to music."
—On her inspiration for songs, *carlyraejepsen.com*

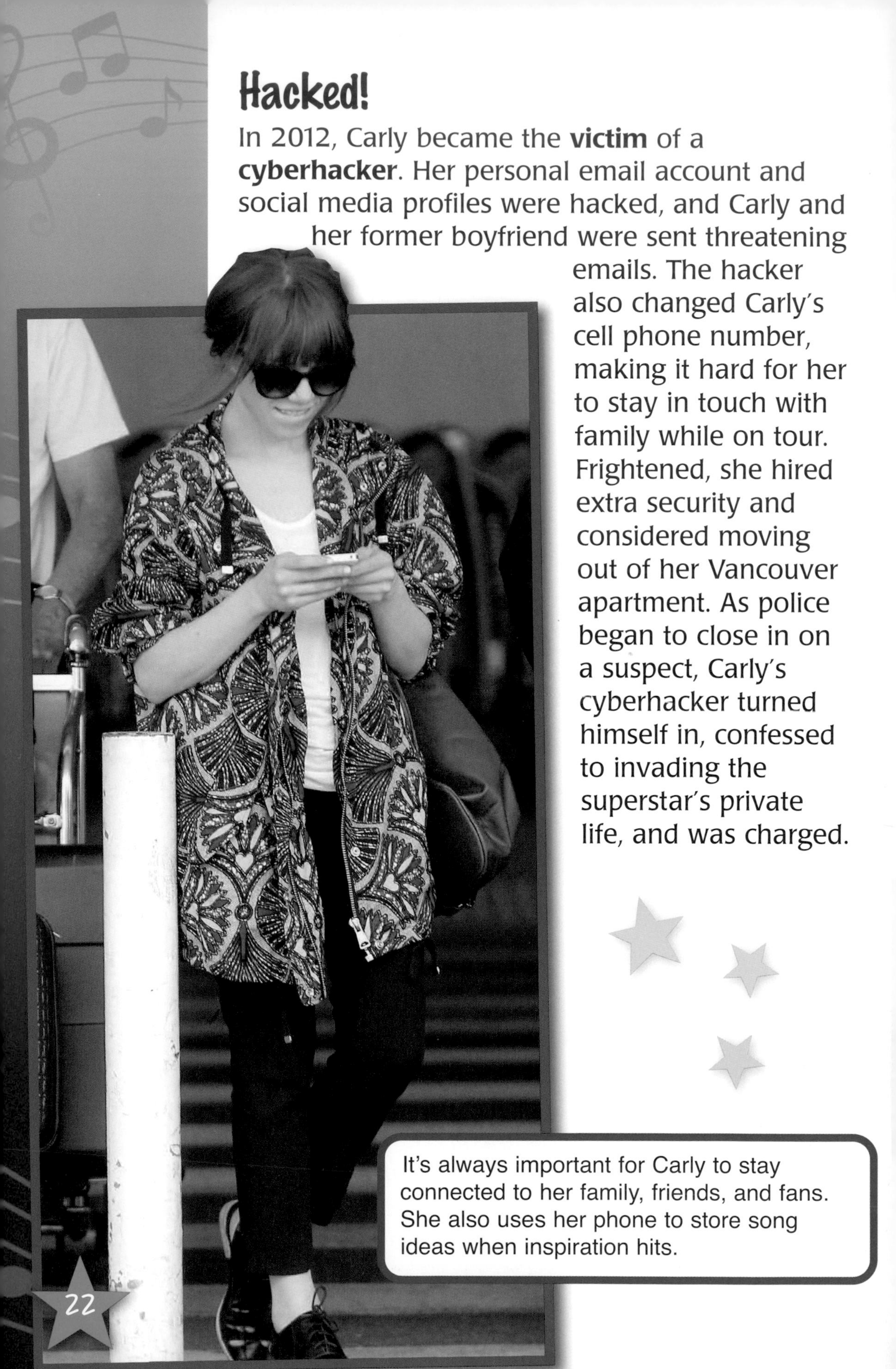

Hacked!

In 2012, Carly became the **victim** of a **cyberhacker**. Her personal email account and social media profiles were hacked, and Carly and her former boyfriend were sent threatening emails. The hacker also changed Carly's cell phone number, making it hard for her to stay in touch with family while on tour. Frightened, she hired extra security and considered moving out of her Vancouver apartment. As police began to close in on a suspect, Carly's cyberhacker turned himself in, confessed to invading the superstar's private life, and was charged.

It's always important for Carly to stay connected to her family, friends, and fans. She also uses her phone to store song ideas when inspiration hits.

Inclusiveness for All

For such a young performer, Carly has shown that she is committed to her beliefs, even when it might hurt her career. In March 2013, she made headlines when she changed her mind about performing at the Boy Scouts of America summer **jamboree** after she learned that the Scouts did not accept homosexual members into the organization. Carly decided she could not support an event that did not include all of her fans. She was praised for her choice by many newspapers and fellow celebrities.

Rocking Out for Bullying Awareness

Later in the year, Carly would help support another cause close to her heart. It was announced she would be headlining an anti-bullying concert in the United States. UniteLIVE: The Concert to Rock Out Bullying is an event that will kick off Bullying Prevention month in October. Carly looks to her older brother Colin as an anti-bullying role model. He always watched out for Carly in school and also stood up for other students being bullied.

In a poster campaign to support National Teen Pregnancy Prevention Month, Carly encourages teen girls to not let their dreams get sidelined.

Fan Favorite

Carly Rae Jepsen is a performer who interacts with her fans and relies on their input. Despite her busy schedule, she is always reaching out to her fans through social media. In a Twitter contest, she shared her love of songwriting with her fans by **crowdsourcing** and having them vote for their favorite song lyrics for the upcoming single "Take a Picture." Before its release, fans could vote for one of three options of lyrics to be recorded in the song. Carly also had her fans choose the name of her 2013 Summer Kiss tour. "Take a Picture" was launched when Carly was featured as a guest judge on an episode of *American Idol.* For Carly, being invited to be a judge on the show was "**surreal**" after having got her start as a contestant on *Canadian Idol*.

PRIMETIME!

Carly made her U.S. television **debut** on the *Ellen* show in 2012 alongside Justin Bieber. She also made a **cameo** appearance on the teenage TV drama, *90210* to perform her new song "This Kiss."

Carly performs her new single "Take a Picture" live on the *American Idol* Season 12 performance show on May 15, 2013.

Summer Kiss Tour

The Summer Kiss tour took Carly to three continents, with shows in Japan, Argentina, Chile, and cities across North America. She was joined by Justin Bieber and pop bands The Wanted and Hot Chelle Rae. When Carly visits foreign countries, she loves experiencing the local food and fashions. She has shopped for kimonos in Japan and gone ziplining through the rainforest in Indonesia.

Carly performs with a flock of colorful dancers at the MTV Music Video Awards in Japan in June 2013.

Beating Out the Biebs

At the 2013 Juno Awards, Carly was nominated for five awards. She went head to head against her **mentor** Justin and beat him out in two categories: best album and best single for "Call Me Maybe." In her acceptance speech, a gracious Carly thanked her fans, calling her wins a "shared success" with Justin.

Take Me Out to the Ball Game!

In 2013, Carly was invited to throw the first pitch at two Major League Baseball games. In April, Carly threw a solid first pitch from the mound at a Baltimore Orioles game. In July, Carly was asked to throw the opening pitch at a home game for the Tampa Bay Rays. Instead of landing in the catcher's mitt, her **erratic** pitch went on a diagonal, knocking a camera out of the hands of a nearby photographer! The pitch was featured in newspapers and television shows as one of the worst first pitches ever thrown! Always a good sport, Carly laughed it off. Her high-energy performance later in the game made up for her missed aim by getting fans on their feet!

SPORTS FAN

Baseball may not be Carly's best sport, but this songbird is a hockey fan. Her favorite National Hockey League team is the Vancouver Canucks.

After throwing the "worst pitch ever," Carly joked through Twitter about making headlines on **ESPN**.

Cover Girl!

Carly has always loved dressing up. As a little girl, she loved wearing tutus so much she even insisted on wearing one on the ski slopes. As she grew up, Carly's fashion sense has matured into a mix of vintage and designer duds. At 5′2″, Carly loves wearing high heels and, in interviews, she often comments on how surprised people are by her height. Carly's sassy style has been featured on the cover of many magazines, including *Seventeen*. She is the current spokesperson for Candie's and has appeared in a commercial for the popular girls' clothing and footwear line. Carly also **endorses** a line of natural beauty products from Burt's Bees, called güd.

Carly was featured as the celebrity judge in *Seventeen's* Pretty Amazing contest. She poses with her cover at a luncheon celebrating the finalists.

Movie Magic

In August 2013, Carly released a special cover of "Part of Your World" from Disney's *The Little Mermaid* to be included on a special DVD release of the movie. Carly was very excited to record the song. In an interview with *Hello!* magazine, she called it a "childhood dream come true" to sing such an **iconic** song from one of her favorite childhood movies. She also got to do a music video for the song. To get into character, Carly decided to dye her hair red to look like Ariel, the little mermaid.

The Exciting Road Ahead

With her runaway success and globetrotting schedule, Carly remains a hometown girl at heart. After a long stretch on the road, she is always happy to spend some quality time with family and friends. Her next project includes working on new songs and recording her third full-length album. Carly has also expressed interest in writing songs for other singers—and maybe even writing a musical! In her personal life, Carly has also said she looks forward to having a family one day. With her amazing success, Carly has proven with hard work, talent, and a little luck, dreams really do come true.

No crowd is too big or small for Carly! In April 2013, Carly blows a kiss to her fans at a high school in Bakersfield, California, that won a free concert through a local radio station.

She Said It

"I have a goal, which is to write that one song that leaves a lasting impression and makes people feel good long after I'm gone. [...] I don't know when it will come or if I'll ever get there, but it would be such an achievement. That's why I get up and do this everyday – to write that song."

—On her continuing goals as an artist, uthmag.com

Timeline

1985: On November 20, Carly Rae Jepsen was born in Mission, British Columbia, Canada

2002: Received her first acoustic guitar and began performing in pubs and cafés

2007: Third-place finish on *Canadian Idol*

2007: Signed to Fontana/Maple-Music in August, then released her first album *Tug of War*

2009: Toured Canada twice with Marianas Trench

2011: Signed to 604 record label

2011: In September "Call Me Maybe" single was released; in December, Justin Bieber and Selena Gomez tweet about the song and it becomes an instant hit

2012: Toured across Canada with Hanson on their Shout It Out World Tour

2012: Became the first official artist signed to School Boy Records and *Curiosity* EP is released on February 14

2012: Toured with Justin Bieber on his Believe tour

2012: Named Rising Star of 2012 at Billboard Music Awards

2012: Second album *Kiss* is released on September 18

2013: Nominated for two Grammy awards; in April, wins Best Album and Best Song of the Year at the Juno Awards

2013: Headlined her Summer Kiss tour

2013: Cover of "Part of Your World" is recorded for *The Little Mermaid* DVD

2013: Headlined the UniteLIVE anti-bullying concert in October

Glossary

cameo A brief appearance of someone famous in a movie or TV show
collaborating Working with someone else
crowdsourcing Obtaining ideas, content, or opinions from a large group of people, especially online or through social media
cyberhacker A person who uses a computer to get access to private information
debut First appearance
endorses Recommends and promotes
EP (extended play) A musical recording that is longer than a single, but shorter than a full album
erratic Wild or crazy
ESPN Entertainment and Sports Programming Network
headlining To be the main performer in a show
iconic Something or someone that is widely recognized
jamboree A large celebration or gathering
label A company that produces music
lyrics The words in a song
mentor Someone who gives help or advice
remixed Changed or added to
parodies Things that imitate something else in a humorous way; often for fun
reggae Traditional Caribbean music sang at a slow tempo
skeptical Uncertain or having doubt
soul A kind of music similar to rhythm and blues which usually expresses lots of emotion
surreal Strange or unusual
tweens Young people between the ages of 10 and 12
unanimous Fully in agreement
victim A person who is cheated, fooled, or harmed by another
viral Describing an image or video that is passed around quickly on the Internet

Find Out More

Books

Higgins, Nadia. *Carly Rae Jepsen: Call Her Amazing*. Lerner Publishing, 2013.

Tieck, Sarah. *Carly Rae Jepsen: Pop Star*. ABDO Publishing, 2013.

Websites

Carly Rae Jepsen
www.carlyraemusic.com
Carly Rae Jepsen's official website

Follow Carly on Twitter
https://twitter.com/carlyraejepsen

Follow Carly on Facebook
https://www.facebook.com/Carlyraejepsen

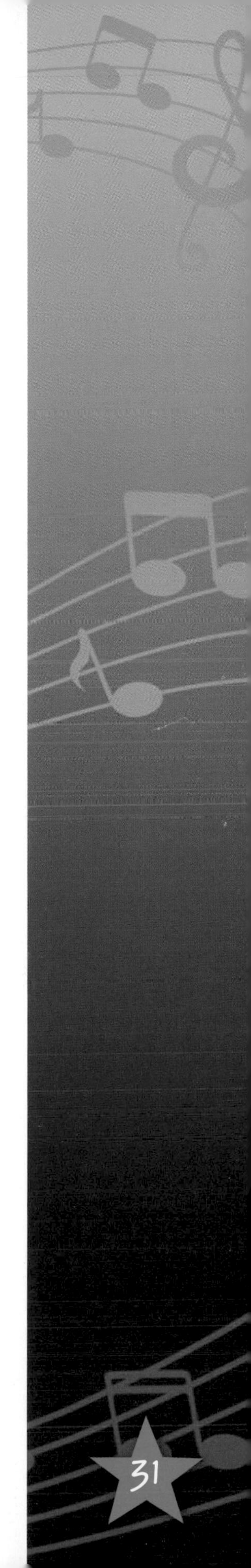

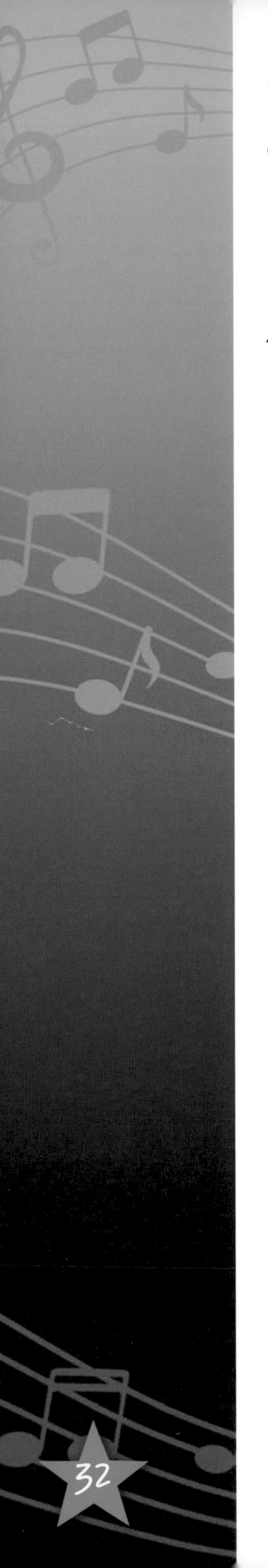

Index

About the Author

Kelly McNiven works as an editor and writer in children's publishing. When her nose is not buried in a book, she enjoys running, cooking vegetarian food, and traveling to new places.